Elizabeth Russell

Creative Collage with Shells & Dried Flowers

Mills & Boon Limited, London

Taplinger Publishing Co. Inc.,
New York

First published in Great Britain 1972 by Mills & Boon Limited,
17–19 Foley Street, London W1A 1DR.
First published in the United States 1973 by Taplinger Publishing Co.
Inc., 200 Park Avenue South, New York, N.Y. 10003.

British ISBN 0.263.05207.9

American ISBN 0–8008–1991–8
Library of Congress Catalog Card Number 72–7216

Made and printed in Great Britain by
Butler & Tanner Ltd, Frome and London

Contents

Note to American readers

The following terms may be unfamiliar to some American readers and are accordingly clarified below to facilitate the use of this book.

Bostik—glue similar to Elmer's glue-all
Fablon—contact paper, vinyl or felt
Fine needlecord—fine corduroy
Hardboard—masonite
Hessian—coarse textured fabric similar to burlap
Notelet box—stationery or note box
Polyfilla—modelling paste, as gesso
Polythene sheeting—plastic sheeting
Snippets—small bits

(1) How to start

It is amazing how many people are suppressed creative artists who are only held back because their taste is better than their talents. They long to create something, make a personal contribution to their homes, express themselves outside the dull routine jobs and mass-produced formula that is, of necessity, a large part of our lives, but then the problems begin. For instance, the sort of picture that most of us could paint would be far below the standards of our taste, and the mistakes that, too late, we see we have made are only possible to correct to a limited degree.

It is true that when using oils corrections can be made by 'over-painting', but after a few alterations the picture becomes muddy, and therefore spoilt. In water colours no errors are possible, and in fact this often despised medium is the hardest to use successfully.

In people who have a high degree of artistic talent there is a wonderful link between eye, hand and inner vision, that enables them to put the brush stroke in exactly the right place, instead of just the wrong one. But it is not a gift given to very many, and even then it must be developed by almost daily practice, which is something for which very few people have the necessary spare time.

These are some of the problems that led to the idea of making these pictures, but I wanted to use the materials in a creative way. I had seen too many groups of brightly-dyed grasses and flowers, stuck together without imagination, to wish to copy that kind of arrangement. There can never be the satisfaction in non-creative work that there is when the imagination is fully involved, even in creating the simplest thing. Talking of being 'creative' may sound rather grand, perhaps even pompous, but if we analyse what it means, it is simply using the imagination on the materials to hand, whatever they may be. After all what is the clay on the potter's wheel but a dull lump of a particular kind of earth, until it is moulded by a deft hand, keen eye and imagination into something of lasting beauty? So when you start to make a picture think of your imagination as the most important requirement, and I hope that these pictures of mine will have the effect of sparking off your imagination in ways personal to you.

The advantage of this kind of picture-making is that you can 'doodle' with your materials until you have them just where you want them; nothing is final till you stick it into place. In fact it is always best, after you have arranged a picture, to go away and come back a little while later. You will then see your picture with fresh eyes, and any mistakes will show up and can be corrected. Another very helpful thing about these pictures is that they can be made in stages, which, because very few people have long periods of free time, is a great advantage. For most of us our spare time comes in snippets, and an odd hour or even half-hour which would be useless to a painter can be used in this kind of picture-making. But more about this as the method is described in the following chapters.

Collecting the materials for these pictures is interesting in itself, a kind of all-the-year-round treasure hunt. There is never a time of year when nothing can be found and stored away against the time when a little leisure makes it possible to begin a picture. All the materials, the shells and dried flowers, etc., are readily available to anyone. Nothing has been used that cannot be grown in a garden or found in the fields and hedgerows or on our beaches.

From the beginning of the year, frost-bleached oak and other leaves can be found, or you can browse comfortably through the seed catalogues planning what you will grow, even if you have only a balcony. Spring, and if you have a garden, or a friend who has one, seeing that the seed heads of the muscari and garden variety of bluebell are not cut down. Later picking up the new growth of the oak tress, so often blown off on very windy days in June, and tucking them into some shrub so that the sun will change them during the summer months to a lovely shade of apricot. Late August and September are the harvesting months; in the garden there will be so many things to collect, and the hedgerows are free to all, and are a happy hunting ground which will add interest to a weekend drive or walk in the country.

When on holiday the same thing applies, and as different beaches have different shells and seaweeds which may even change from day to day, it is fun to visit several and see what treasures each can provide. The only ones not worth a visit are those covered with large pebbles, because any shells that are washed up will get broken on these shores. The children too can join in the treasure hunt, and if many of the shells they find are not suitable for your pictures, don't throw them away, for at the end of this book I have given some suggestions for ways in which children can make 'fun' pictures and other things with these shells.

The last but not least advantage of these pictures, is that apart from most of the materials being free from the garden or countryside, the other constituents are cheap. Hardboard which is used for the backing will cost very little. The rayons, cottons and velveteens for the background covering are not expensive either, and as the amount required is small it can often be found on the remnant counter, another aspect of the treasure hunt. All the equipment is simple, consisting of household or very ordinary articles. Here is the list of what you will need:

An old blunt kitchen knife.
A pair of rat-nosed pliers (long-ended, narrowing to $\frac{1}{4}$ inch).
Millinery pins, and some ordinary ones.
Tailor's chalk (white).
$\frac{1}{2}$ inch decorator's paint brush.
A small pair of scissors (old ones will do).
A clear fixative; I use UHU.
Polyfilla.
Sandpaper.
An old cup.
Plasticine

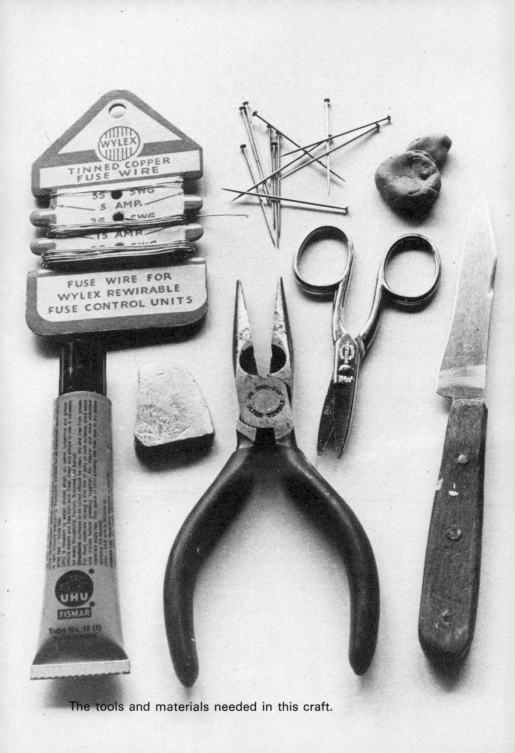

The tools and materials needed in this craft.

So no big expense is involved until the picture is framed, and even here there are ways of reducing the cost, as I shall explain when describing the special method of framing that is needed. But as framing is the last thing to be done, obviously only your successful pictures will reach that stage, so you won't need to worry if you should have less than complete success with your first effort. Perhaps because you don't have to worry you will have successes right from the start. It may be of interest to know that there is quite a history behind this collage method of picture-making. There was a lady in the eighteenth century who was famous for the charm and delicacy of her fern pictures, and nearer to our own time both Queen Mary and Mr Oliver Messel are reputed to have enjoyed making such pictures. Collages have been made of a wide variety of things, so much so that it can be a pitfall. I am convinced that only by being both creative and selective will a higher standard of picture be achieved, so that perhaps at some future time they will be prized as examples of the handicraft of our day, and show that in a mass-produced age there were still creative individualists.

(2) What to look for—plant life

The first thing to remember is that everything must be durable. These pictures are not made to last for just a few months, but for years. Several of mine are now fifteen or more years old and show no signs of change, loss of colour, or any other deterioration. Whatever you collect and dry must be shaken before you use it in a picture; this applies particularly to dried seed heads. Wherever it is possible let nature do the drying, as she does it so well. Anything that has withstood bleaching by sun and frost, and drying by winds, has a high degree of durability, and will not easily disintegrate.

When you search for materials, whether on the seashore or in the hedgerows, fields and garden, look for beauty of shape, and the possibility of creating new forms in alliance with other flowers, seed heads, shells and seaweeds. Not only what they are but what you can create with them, should be the constant idea in your mind. There will be further details and suggestions in the section on design.

There are two main varieties of oak tree to be found growing wild. Look for the kind with the very indented leaves, after hard frosts have bleached them a creamy-beige, or when they have been torn down by summer winds and turned apricot colour by the sun. Ivy, though an evergreen, sheds some of its leaves at various times of year. They should be collected when they have become cream-coloured; the small 'three-fingered' ivy is an especially pretty shape.

All leaves should be placed on a sheet of newspaper for the final dry-out, which must be done very slowly; quick drying will make them curl up. If this should happen, or you find otherwise attractive leaves too curled up, make them very damp, put them between layers of newspaper, with just enough thickness in the upper layer to hold them down without pressing them flat (this takes away the

(Opposite) Some of the 'raw' materials gathered from garden and countryside.

look of life and movement). Bracken should be gathered when it is
golden. Sometimes a spray will turn this colour as early as August.
It will darken as it dries, so do not wait till it is rather brown.
Dry as described for other leaves.

Hornbeam seeds with bugles and beads.

Cow parsley seed head with sequins.

Beads with sequin centre. Queen Anne's lace.

Hornbeam seeds have many uses and can be arranged singly or in
groups, perhaps with a bright-coloured bead replacing the seed.
These can be collected in the autumn as can the seed heads of
cow parsley and Queen Anne's lace, which are rather alike, though
as the name suggests, Queen Anne's lace is more delicate in shape
and smaller in size. Gather the cow parsley seed heads at different
stages, some while the heads are still slightly green and full of
seeds. Flatten the head a little very gently, and leave to dry on a
sheet of newspaper with a few more thicknesses to hold it down,
but again without pressing it flat. For these pictures nothing should
ever be pressed quite flat, it makes things look stiff and mummified.

When the head is dry spray with hair-setting lotion to 'fix' the seeds. For a different effect pick some heads with no seeds on them or very few, flatten slightly, dry and spray as before. These look lovely with sequins stuck onto the little claw-like tops which held the seeds, where they make a shining substitute. A mixed head of real seeds and some sequins is very attractive, particularly if gold, bronze or pearl-coloured ones are used.

Skeleton leaves are lovely too, making a soft web to connect up more solid shapes; experiment with holly, ivy, magnolia, poplars, but especially magnolia leaves, which can often be found in skeleton form. If you cannot find any in this delicate state of decay it is possible to make them by artificial means, and I will give the necessary recipe at the end of the book.

Helichrysum flowers with separate petals.

Helichrysum can be grown in the garden, or bought at a florist's. They come in a lovely range of colours as well as having varied uses. If you buy them look for the bunch with the flowers that are least opened, and if you are picking them from the garden gather them when they first come into bloom, because every type of flower opens more as it is being dried. For these pictures only the flower heads are needed, and they can be cut off separately as they come into bloom. Then lay them on a piece of paper to dry in a cool room. This way there is no risk of the heads becoming misshapen by being pressed against other blooms as they dry. A few can be dried on a sunny window sill; this will make them open more fully till the petals become reflexed, and the boss of stamens shows as a raised yellow cushion. They are very effective when combined with a circle of individual petals from another flower, especially if these are bright yellow or flame red.

Should you wish to dry the helichrysums so that they can be used for flower arrangements or pictures, cut off all the leaves (do not pull them off because that weakens the stem), then thread a wire through the stalk and hang them in a cool but dry place, keeping each group of flower heads well apart.

Helichrysum with honesty.

Another charming flower can be created by using a fairly small helichrysum for the centre with one or more rows of honesty for the outer petals. The latter is a very easily grown biennial. It should be gathered in late September or early October before bad weather can

(Opposite)
Helichrysum, honesty, fronds of bracken and gypsophila combine to make this very modern picture. Individual florets of hydrangea with sequins in the centres, and a scattering of bronze sequins, link the main groups together.

batter the seed pods, but not until they are beginning to turn brown. This dull sheath is removed by lifting the brown layer at the stalk end to reveal the shining white inner section, to which the seeds adhere, but only lightly. If you scatter these seeds they will usually grow and produce the plants you want for the following year.

 Anaphalis with beads and petals of helichrysum or with petals and seed boss replaced by a bead or pearl.

An easily-grown hardy herbaceous plant whose flowers are 'everlasting' is Anaphalis, either trilinervis or margaritacea, both varieties having small clusters of tiny daisy-like flowers with silver-green foliage. They are an asset to the garden as well as to these pictures. They bloom in August, but their long-lasting flowers stay on to make a lovely foil to the mauves of the Michaelmas daisies. The silver-white flowers can be used in groups, or separately, ringed with individual petals of a helichrysum. They also look lovely scattered like stars, especially if the picture has a deep-coloured back covering. Pick them when they first come into flower, and dry them by pushing the stalks through some fine wire netting, so that the head of flowers rests on the wire and the stalk hangs down. As before a cool and dry place is needed for drying, and with this method they can be used for both pictures and flower arrangements.

(Opposite)
This is an example of a lovely effect with simple means. Long strands of the bleached grass found in the winter hedgerows, curving out from the central group of helichrysum and honesty. Tiny anaphalis flowers are scattered over the purple-blue background, some having yellow helichrysum petals set round them, and contrasting beads in the centre of all the flowers.

Molucella (bells of Ireland) stuck to a stalk of grass, a sequin added.

Bells of Ireland (Molucella) are not so easy to grow as they are half-hardy annuals, but are worth the extra trouble. They should be picked when the bells feel a little dry to the touch, but as they flower rather late in the summer, they may not be ready before the frost. If this happens protect the spikes with polythene bags. This also applies to hydrangeas. Dry them by passing a wire through the stalks and hang them as before in a cool, dry place, but please note that a garage is neither, once the cooler weather begins. If you haven't a suitable shed or spare room, the loft is a better place. The kitchen is not suitable, being too warm and steamy. Occasionally the green colour of the bells is retained after drying, but usually they become a soft cream shade. One effective way of using them is to stick single bells along an arching stem of grass, or to thin out a head of oats, cutting away the seed husk and replacing it with a bell. If a vivid coloured bead is stuck in place so that it looks as if it is hanging out of the bell, this adds to its attractiveness.

Muscari are easy happy flowers and dry themselves into a spray of tiny bells if you don't cut them back when they have finished flowering; they will thus also seed themselves. They will be dry and sunbleached by July or early August. Cut off the back seed pods, i.e. back in relation to how you want to use them, shape the stalks if needed by damping and gently curving them into a good line;

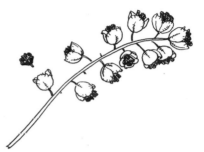

Florets of statice added to seed cases of muscari.

then pin them onto a piece of paper and leave to dry again. They combine very well with statice, which though it comes in several pretty colours, is not a good shape. The mauve and rose-red are the two best shades. Cut out the flowers with small pointed scissors, then dip the ends of the tiny flowers in UHU and stick them into the equally tiny bells of the muscari. The effect is a new and lovely flower, graceful in shape and with beautiful touches of colour.

Seed head of clematis tangutica with pearl centre and beads.

The seed heads of clematis tangutica have a fairy-like quality. They can be collected while still slightly green, then placed on a window-sill to dry. The centre may need to be secured with a little UHU applied with a millinery pin, or sprayed with hair-setting lotion. When using them in a picture a single pearl or diamanté crystal fixed in the centre with more glue looks lovely against the silver-grey hairs of the seed wings, and also holds them firmly in place. The wild clematis, commonly called Old Man's Beard, can be used in a similar way.

Floret and single petals of hydrangea made into a new flower.

There are two methods of drying hydrangeas, but first it is essential to pick them at the right time, when they are papery to the touch. Obviously the time will vary according to when they came into flower, but it is usually about mid- or late September, so beware of frosts, and cover them with polythene bags at night if you want them to retain their colour, because frost will bleach them. Both methods of drying require that you cut the stalk between the joints from which the leaves grow, and pull off the leaves. Put them in a vase in half an inch of water and either leave them in a cool room or put them in the linen cupboard for four days. Both methods have about the same proportion of successes; the advantage of the latter method is that you know the rate of success sooner. The heads last equally well either way. The red shades last best and the greenish ones quite well, but the blues tend to fade. Whole heads are too large to use, but individual florets, or a flower made up of separate petals with a floret in the centre, produce a charming effect, rather like a carnation.

Cape gooseberries can be made into a striking flower if the seed head is cut down the 'join' with a razor blade, till the sections can lie almost flat. A small cream or yellow helichrysum, or poppy seed head, will make an attractive centre to this new lily-like flower.

I cannot name all the seed heads, flowers, leaves and grasses that can be used to make these pictures, indeed if I did some of the fun would be lost, for it is in hunting, finding, and creating with what you find, that half the pleasure and all the art lies.

Treasures from the seashore.

(3) What to look for on the seashore

There are two standards for seashore treasures, either perfect and unblemished, or worn and changed by the action of sea and sand into some new fantastic shape. The best beaches are sandy ones; a rocky shore breaks up all but the largest and toughest shells. Each beach seems to have its own speciality, though a storm may bring in quite a new range of shells. Sometimes one part of a beach is always better than another, and very often the best shells are half-buried in the sand.

Oyster shells are perhaps the queen of the beach; some worn so thin that they are translucent by, no one knows how many years of tossing in sea and on the sand, yet still strong. They are a natural for creating fantastic sea flowers, in fact it was finding some of these shells that first made me want to create shell pictures. They can be found on the shores of Cornwall, Dorset or any sandy beaches that are in the Colchester area, though they are sometimes washed up elsewhere. If you do happen to be in France, and so many people do go abroad these days, Brittany and Vendée are the best places, and the northern coast of Brittany better than the southern part.

Mussels, small ones, can be used with the blueish inside showing, but they are surprisingly frail and must be handled with care.
Of course see that all shells are empty, and wash them well before bringing them home or you may find yourself with more ozone than you want!

Sea urchin decorated with beads and edged with tiny venus shells.

Very large shells are useless for these pictures. They would need too much depth for practical or pleasing framing. But if nice large shells come your way, or the children collect them, look at the end of this book for ways of using them.

Search for the beautiful small shells at the incoming tide line, as then they are less likely to be broken. It is also a help to search with your back to the sun, as it will often pick out the gleam of a half-buried shell that you would not have seen with the sun shining in your eyes.

It really is a hunt, but so fascinating that once started you are likely to become a confirmed beachcomber, hardly bothering with such dull ordinary things as basking and bathing! There are an amazing variety of shells to be found, including tiny specimens of larger kinds. I have variegated scallop shells only a $\frac{1}{4}$-inch across yet perfect in form and colour. (The full size is $1\frac{1}{2}$ inches or more.) Lobe shells, Atlantic coquina, smooth venus and striped venus, ark shells, top shells, periwinkles, to list but a few, are common round our shores, and many more that according to books on the subject, should not by rights be here at all. That is the advantage of having an Atlantic coast line.

Many of these shells are in lovely colours, ranging from yellow to orange, mauve, blue and pink shades, others are the purest white which can make an effective contrast to a bright-coloured background, and highlight the shape of the shell. A small point of interest about the Atlantic coquina, which is usually found joined at the 'hinge', is that if it is not found joined together you will never match two shells exactly, the marking and colours are as individual to each pair of shells as fingerprints.

Atlantic coquina with bugles and beads on wire for body.

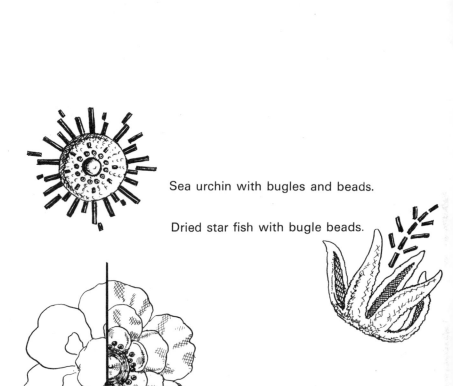

Sea urchin with bugles and beads.

Dried star fish with bugle beads.

Method of building up oyster shell flower, with top shell centre and stamens, fixed with Polyfilla.

European cowrie shells with stalk of sea-holly and small mussel shells.

Two pieces of spirula stuck in reverse position.

Small striped cockle shells with group of small barnacles in the centre.

Smooth white venus shells with dark variegated top shell in the centre and bronze sequins. The barnacles and top shell must be stuck with a little Polyfilla.

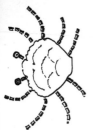

Crab shells with bugles and beads.

Atlantic coquina often striped and in a wide range of colours. Here with tiny scallop shell.

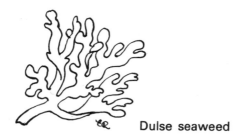

Dulse seaweed

Top shells can often be found with the conical point worn off, revealing the coloured spiral of pearl inside. In this state they make a lovely centre for a flower of oyster shells, with perhaps a circle of stamens. These are made of fine gold-coloured wire or fuse wire, cut into one-inch lengths onto which a bright-coloured bead is threaded. Then the wire is doubled back and twisted to keep the bead in place.

The shells, or cases, of sea-urchins can quite often be found on the Cornish or Welsh coasts, but are most plentiful on Mediterranean beaches. With their natural pattern picked out in orange or turquoise beads they also make an attractive centre for a flower, and look effective with bugles of jet sticking out all round where their stings would be.

Of the flotsam and jetsam, the oddest and loveliest is a queer kind of hair seaweed that collects and holds fast to masses of tiny or broken bits of shells. I have walked along a beach at the high-tide line where so many of these strands have been washed up, that they looked like rows of necklaces and bracelets. I might add that at another time on the same beach there were none; that is one of the strange things about beachcombing, you never know what a tide will bring. When they can be found they can be arranged in very many ways, as they curve or group at the user's will, and are easily fixed in place with glue. Another oddity is the tiny starfish that have dried out after being stranded above the high-tide line, and curled up till they look like an exotic flower.

Seaweed is another very useful high-tide-line-find, but often almost completely buried in the sand, and bleached to the same colour. It cannot be bleached at home, so don't bring home damp slimy stuff and hope to change it. All it will do is to tell you if the weather will be wet or dry.

There is an interesting dark brown seaweed that is often found dried into tangled balls. If you find some in this condition don't despair of using it. When you get home soak it well in cold water till it is pliable enough to unravel, then spread it out on newspaper into the shapes you want, pinning it down by sliding millinery pins across the stalk part, and leave to dry very slowly. Sometimes it is found with a group of tiny barnacles growing onto it which can make either the basic part of a design, or an attractive addition to it, so keep your eyes open for such oddities.

I never mix the things I find on the sea-shore with those I find in fields and garden, they seem a world apart. What I have described are only a few of the fascinating things you can find, and with which you can evoke the idea of a special and strange kind of garden from the sea.

(4) Covering the backing

In the first chapter I said that one of the advantages of these pictures was that they could be made in stages according to the amount of free time, and also inclination. For storing in between, a cardboard box will be needed, large enough to hold the picture with ease so that it can be lifted in and out without damage. If there is likely to be a long time in between opportunities for making the picture, it should be put in a polythene bag as well, with a clip round the neck of the bag so that it balloons out, and does not rest on the picture.

I don't think that men have any more free time than women, but they often have the advantage of having their spare time in larger 'lumps'. For the housewife her home is also her office, the cooker her desk, and the kitchen sink the in-and-out tray. So do realise when reading the instructions which I shall be giving in the following chapters, that each stage can be done separately, and that when some item must be done at one time I will make that clear.

For the backing nothing is cheaper or easier to handle than hardboard. Anyone can cut it to the required size, but should you prefer, any Do-It-Yourself shop will cut it for you. After some trial and error fabrics proved to have many advantages as a covering. The range of colours and textures is wide, and therefore finding just the shade to suit a room is likely to be easy. Another reason for using fabrics is that they 'key-in' so well with the two fixatives needed, Polyfilla and UHU, and with the dried materials, and the shells. There are only a few don'ts: real silk, apart from being expensive, is very much affected by atmospheric changes, and a covering that was tight and smooth, may well sag on a damp day. Hessian is clumsy to handle and will be bulky at the corners, so that when the picture is framed it may make problems. All the rayons, rayon and cotton mixtures, cotton velvet, velveteens and fine needlecords are excellent. Velveteen, both plain and needlecord, is especially suitable for shell pictures if a water effect is to be created with the 'wave line'. Tie-dye can also give lovely effects, particularly when allied with large groups of shells or the more solid flower or leaf shapes. Cotton, and rayon and cotton mixtures, are some of the fabrics which respond well to this method.

When choosing the colour of the covering fabric, do bear in mind that the contrast between the colour of the fabric and that of the shells and dried flowers being used, will make half the effectiveness of the picture. For instance yellow and cream shells or flowers would not show to as much advantage on a pale yellow or beige background, as they would on turquoise blue or clear green. Another point to remember is that glass has a slightly dimming effect, so do not choose too muted a tone of the colour of your choice.

Now for the first stage in your picture-making; covering the hard-board. This must be done properly, for it is just as important to do this correctly, as it is to prepare a canvas or the paper for a water-colour picture, though very much easier.

First cut the fabric two inches larger all round than the size of the hardboard, and over-sew the edges, as frayed ends are a nuisance when sticking the fabric to the board. Mark both the board and the fabric with tailor's chalk to indicate the top of the picture. This is especially important when a square or nearly square picture is being made, and a fabric with a marked weave or nap is used for the covering. Velveteen can have the pile running up or down, but must never run from side to side. Always draw a thread to cut along.

Place the hardboard, smooth side down, onto the centre of the fabric, turn over the edges and mitre the corners. Pin in place, making sure that the weave of the fabric is in line with the edge of the board. Sew the mitred corners in place, stitching first up and then down, so that the effect is a crossed stitch (see diagrams). Using UHU, run some under the edge of the turning, press down evenly, and leave to dry; this only takes a few minutes (see diagram). Next stick the opposite side, checking as you press the fabric down that the weave is straight and smooth on the front

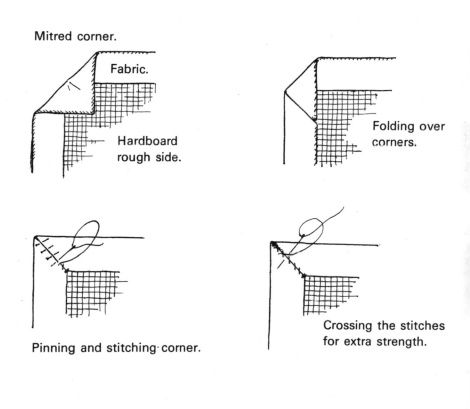

Mitred corner.

Fabric.

Hardboard
rough side.

Folding over
corners.

Pinning and stitching corner.

Crossing the stitches
for extra strength.

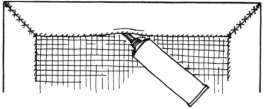

Running the glue under the edge of the fabric.

COVERING THE HARDBOARD

side. Again leave to dry. Continue with the next side, always checking that the weave is straight, and when the last side is being stuck, take special care that the fabric is taut and smooth, with no 'bubbles' on the front surface of the picture. On *no* account try to stick the fabric to the smooth front surface of the hardboard. It is next to impossible to make it lie taut and smooth, though in theory this would seem to be the obvious method.

If the water-wave-line effect is wanted, as shown in the illustration on page 45, or the effect in the picture on page 69, a slightly different procedure must be followed, and the best fabrics to choose are cotton velvets and plain or fine needlecord velveteens. Cut and oversew as described before, pin into place on the board, then run a tacking thread where the edge of the picture will be. Un-pin the fabric and remove from the board. Put it in a bowl of cold water till it is thoroughly wet—this will take several minutes as velvet does not absorb water quickly—then lay it flat on a sheet of poly-thene. Have ready a cup of well-dissolved dye, choosing either a darker shade of the background colour, or one which will produce a contrasting colour. Blue dye used on yellow will make blue-green waves, blue on rose-red will give a wine purple effect. The colour of the background must always be taken into account, and it is a good practice to test out the effect of the dye on an odd scrap of the fabric.

(Opposite)
The 'wave' line is used to evoke the idea of a sea garden. The large flowers are made of oyster shells, with centres of top shells which have been reshaped by the sea. Tiny groups of barnacles make the centres of the other flowers, ringed by petals of white tellin. The variegated shells have made a long sea journey, but Atlantic coasts provide many surprises. Dulse seaweed is common to our shores, but the fine fronds of molgula are more rare.

(Below) Both a picture and a beautiful tray.

(Opposite) Some common and unusual seed heads are arranged together in this picture – cow parsley, Queen Anne's lace, bells of Ireland, muscari seed heads with individual flowers cut from statice, and sequins to provide touches of sparkling colour. Sprays of dried asparagus fern, set with hair lacquer, add a softening effect.

Then if you feel very sure that you know exactly where you want the wave-lines, paint them in using a big water-colour brush, direct onto the fabric. But if you prefer to be careful and not risk mistakes, cut some short lengths of sewing cotton and arrange them till they are exactly where you want the wave-lines, then paint the dye along beside the thread lines, lift them off, and widen the line as much as you wish.

Should you want to create the effect shown in the picture on page 45, it is essential to use the lengths of sewing cotton because for this ordinary bleach is used at full strength. As bleach is colourless, it will not show up on the wet fabric where the waves have been painted until the bleaching has begun, so without the sewing cotton there would be no guide lines.

The length of time the bleaching takes will depend on the strength of the light, and the degree of change desired. If it is attempted at night it will take some hours, so it is always advisable to do this process during the day. When the desired change has been reached, rinse thoroughly in cold water, and during both methods keep the fabric lying flat while it is drying. Double shade effects can be achieved by painting a second line of bleach at the edge of the first, after it has started to change colour. The degree of shade contrast will depend on how much bleaching has taken place in the first application before the second one is applied, and also of course at what point rinsing is done, for this stops the bleaching process.

One point about this process which must always be borne in mind, is the fugitive nature of blue in colour combinations, and as it is one of the primary colours it is a part of many other colours. For instance if bleach is applied to green-coloured fabric, the blue of the blue and yellow that makes green will go, leaving a line of yellower green. If used on mauve a pinkish shade will be left.

On a light but clear blue-green velvet the double line method produces some beautiful water effects. It is also very lovely when used on emerald green, evoking the image of an under-water scene.

(5) Designing a picture/Use of fixatives

There are two ways of working out a design, the pinning-up method, and the rough-out on graph paper, but the latter has to be used only in conjunction with wave-water-lines or tie-dyed backgrounds. A slightly different method is needed for shell pictures and will be described separately.

So let us begin with the pinning-up method. Have a box or tray with a good selection of dried flowers, leaves and grasses beside you, and start to arrange them on your covered board, changing them this way and that, till you feel satisfied with what you see. Then slide pins across the stalks into the fabric, or slip them in vertically to hold leaves or flowers in place. At first, aim only to pin up the main shapes, the 'bones' of the picture. This principle of design applies to painting just as much as it does to these pictures.

Personally I never fix anything at once, but go away so that I get a fresh-eyed look at it when I come back. I also make a point of viewing it from a distance.

Here I would like to make a few suggestions about design, and also illustrate them with diagrams, as I think it is something that can best be comprehended visually.

Many things go to make up a good design, colour contrasts and blending, variation of shapes, the use of solid masses in juxtaposition to fragile ones. Aim to draw the eye from object to object in the picture, smoothly and gracefully, though this does not mean that a design should be pretty-pretty. Selectiveness is another very important factor, which up to a point has to be a matter of personal taste. For instance, I never use dyed flowers or grasses, or varnished shells, because I dislike their harsh, unnatural look, and have reason to doubt their lasting qualities. But it cannot be set down as an unbreakable rule of good selection.

When you are satisfied that things are where you want them, lightly mark their places on the fabric with tailor's chalk, making a circle for flowers. As you unpin them put the ones you are going to use aside in another box or tray, otherwise you will have difficulty in finding the exact pieces again. If you have only a little free time available, unpin one group at a time, and stick it as soon as it is unpinned, always remembering that if a stalk or leaf lies partly over another, the under one must be stuck first, and that when creating any of the flowers suggested in Chapters 2 and 3, you must start at the outer edge and work towards the centre.

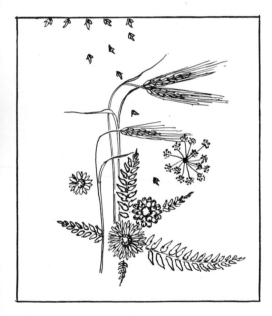

WRONG DESIGN
The same items are used in both pictures. The faults of this design are that pliable materials have not been used to the best advantage. The main items are set squarely, there is no sense of movement, and many lines are repeated awkwardly.

37

Buy the smaller size tube of UHU as it has a finer nozzle, and with care the glue can be applied direct onto leaves, stalks of barley and oats, and all the larger items. But a millinery pin should be used to apply the glue to small things, or fine things, such as the ail or awn of barley, which is the name of the whiskered sides. If these are spread out it gives them the appearance of being blown in the wind. Dip one millinery pin in the glue and run it along the awn, *after* the main stalk has been stuck, then lightly with another

RIGHT DESIGN
Here the pliable materials have been made to curve so that they complement and harmonise. The awn of the barley has been stuck to give a look of grace and movement. The hornbeam seeds float down connecting areas of the design together. Helichrysum, bracken and cow parsley complete the picture.

pin guide the awn into place and press down lightly with a finger. The same method is used when putting beads into the centre of flowers, or sequins onto seed heads. In fact, whenever two tiny pointed fingers are needed, I find millinery pins much more use than tweezers.

Amongst the dried materials helichrysums are one of the few things that must be fixed with Polyfilla, as they are too rough-backed to hold securely with glue. First cut away the back petals with the small scissors. This reduces the depth of the flower and also makes them easier to stick in place. Mix a little Polyfilla (about two teaspoonsful) to the consistency of soft butter with cold water, then, with a blunt kitchen knife, work a little well into the fabric where the circle for the flower has been marked. Then spread some onto the back of the helichrysum. Press lightly in place with a finger or pencil in the centre of the flower, holding it there for a moment or two.

When fixing individual petals of helichrysums or honesty, pass the base section over the nozzle of the UHU, squeezing the tube very gently. Then, having already marked the circle where they are to be placed (for this draw round a coin with tailor's chalk) press them down with either the blunt end of a pencil, or for honesty use a finger-tip. Don't put glue all over the surface of the honesty, it will look much more alive if only part is stuck down, and it will also help if one or two of the seed cases are slightly curled at the outer edges.

Sequins play a rather special part in these pictures. Though I would urge that they should be used with good taste and restraint, they do help to 'join' sections of a design. Both sequins and individual petals of helichrysum can be arranged so that they drift from one group to another, gracefully linking them together, and giving a look of movement and life to the picture.

Simplicity and charm combine to make a lovely tray.

'Into something rich and strange.'

The special method needed for some shells

Many shells and most seaweeds can be held in place while the design is being worked out, by slipping a pin vertically, or sideways, but as I am sure you will realise, this is not practical in the case of many curved shells, or the lovely oyster shells that are used to form flowers.

The latter are found in two main shapes, one which is almost flat, and can often be used unchanged for the back petals of a flower. The other is curved, sometimes so much so that to use it without some shaping would be difficult or even impossible. Both from the design point of view, and for testing during shaping, something is needed that will hold the shells in place, and I have found no better answer to this problem than cream-coloured Plasticine. But please may I make it quite clear that the Plasticine is used to hold the shell temporarily instead of pins. It is *not a fixative*.

Mould a piece of Plasticine to about the size of a 10p piece, and a $\frac{1}{4}$ inch thick, but this will vary according to the size of the flower you wish to make. Sort out the oyster shells, taking care that they blend together well. It surprises many people to find that these shells can be found in a range of colours from creamy-white, through golden to orange and black.

Press the chosen shells into the Plasticine, noting how they lie. Some will need quite a lot of shaping if the hinge end is very curved over, while others may need little or no shaping. For those that must be shaped, hold the shell *very* firmly between the forefinger and thumb, and with a pair of rat-nosed or long-ended pliers very carefully nibble away the curved-up end. As you do this the forefinger must be moved along, so that it is supporting the part of the shell being shaped. Test frequently by putting the shell back into the Plasticine, so that you do not make a mistake and nibble off too much. The small areas can be rounded off with sandpaper. Incidentally, cream-coloured Plasticine and plain-headed pins are

SHAPING OYSTER SHELLS

The line shows at what point the shell has to be shaped.

Holding the shell to be shaped; note forefinger position.

Showing how the shell is 'nibbled' away by the pliers.

These points may need to be rubbed down with sandpaper.

Testing out the shells in Plasticine for shape and fit, *not* as a fixative.

used because any touch of colour that will not be in the final design can distract the eye, and confuse the concept of the picture.

Arrange and re-arrange the shells till they rest in the Plasticine as naturally as petals, then decide what you will use for the centre of the flower. I use a variety of things, top shells, usually those that have had the point worn away, also very small oyster shells clustering round the bright yellow or orange of a flat-sided periwinkle. Often when using a top shell centre I add a ring of stamens. The way to make these was described in Chapter 3.

Whatever your choice, it is easy, with the shell flower held in the Plasticine 'holder', to move it about on the covered board, till it is placed most effectively in relation to the other shells and seaweed that are being used in the picture. Mark round the flower with tailor's chalk, and mark the other items as well. Should any chalk mark show after an item has been stuck in place, brush the chalk away with the small decorator's brush. This is quite easy, though it should be done with care.

Fixing a shell flower in place is one of those occasions when it is important to have a completely free half an hour, even to the point of ignoring the telephone. Though I say half an hour, I can usually manage in ten or fifteen minutes, but at first a longer time should be allowed. Of course have all the chosen items ready, shells shaped, and stamens made, if they are to be used. But remember the sorting and choosing can be done on one day, and the fixing at quite another time, thus shortening the length of time when you must concentrate.

First remove the shells from the Plasticine, laying them out on a tray in exactly the same order. Mix the Polyfilla with cold water to the consistency of soft butter, and, with the blunt knife, work some well into the fabric in the centre of the place marked for the flower. Then build it up to the same size and thickness as the Plasticine 'holder'. Now stick the oyster shells into the Polyfilla in exactly

Helichrysums and honesty combine to make strange new flowers.

The 'pearl' of sea shells gleaming in natural beauty.

the same order and way as they were before, always starting at the outer edge if more than one row of shells is being used (see diagram, page 25). Finish by gently pressing the centre shell into place, and sticking the stamens into the slight bulge of Polyfilla that results from the pressure. Place the picture flat until it has dried. This will take between five and ten minutes, depending on the warmth of the room.

WRONG DESIGN
The eye is pulled from object to object, without harmony or balance. Exactly the same items are used in both pictures—shells, seaweed, crab, sea urchin, beads and sequins.

Oyster shells, which are of course coated inside with the substance from which pearls are made, polish beautifully if rubbed between the finger and thumb, and judging by my pictures the lovely gleam lasts. Wealthy women who owned necklaces of real pearls are said to have slept in them, as the oils from the human skin added to the lustre of the pearls as nothing else could, hence the value of rubbing the shells between the finger and thumb.

RIGHT DESIGN
In this the eye is led from group to group, which, while having shape value in themselves, contribute to the whole design. The sequins add to the linking of the groups or separate objects.

The graph-paper method is only needed when either the water-wave-line, or the tie-dye background is used. The reason for this is that the main arrangement of dried materials or shells must be decided upon before the wave-line or the tie-dyeing is done, if it is to fit properly and effectively into the design.

Cut the graph paper to the same size as the picture, and arrange the materials on it, marking the places with a pencil when you are satisfied with the design; as before put the chosen materials in a separate box or tray. Then place lengths of sewing cotton on the paper to indicate the wave-line or areas for tie-dyeing, arranging them to fit in with the design already outlined; mark the position of the cotton with a pencil.

This provides a plan to work from, and as graph paper is squared, it is reasonably easy with the help of these measurements to draw on the fabric with tailor's chalk, where the dyeing or bleaching is to be carried out. Obviously the background must be done first, and when the process described in Chapter 4 is finished, and the fabric dry, the hardboard can then be covered.

Then using the graph paper as a map of the design, whether of dried materials or shells, and with the aid of a ruler to check distances, it is not difficult to transfer the marked areas and lines to exactly the same places on the covered hardboard, using tailor's chalk.

(Opposite)

The vivid colour of the background is used to throw into sharp relief the shapes of tiny cockle shells, spirula, sea urchins and odd pieces of flotsam and jetsam. Jet bugles and black sequins are effective links and additions.

(Above) These could be lovely poppies from a sea garden.

(Above opposite)
This close-up shows in detail how by combining the separate petals of a helichrysum with one that is fully opened, a new flower can be created.

(Below opposite)
A close-up showing the effectiveness of replacing some of the seeds on a head of cow parsley with sequins. Small helichrysums are used to give colour contrasts.

Atlantic coquina, the 'butterfly' shell.

The smaller shells are fixed with UHU. If the curved side of the shell is used uppermost, which is generally the case as it is the more ornamental side, run a little UHU round under the edge of the shell, then press it down into place on the fabric. Tiny crab shells of various species can often be found; some are white while others are in every shade of coral. The hollow inside should be filled with Polyfilla to strengthen them, smoothing it off so that it is flush with the edge of the shell, before leaving to dry. Stick them into place with UHU with perhaps a bead added for eyes, and a few more arranged to look like claws.

If the curved side of the shell is to be used next to the fabric, put the glue onto the shell at the point of contact with the background, and gently press in place. Tellins are sometimes used in this way, and there are tiny white shells with a pearly inside which are obviously much more effective if used with this side showing. Where beads or sequins are needed stick these items as described in Chapter 5.

One other point about shell pictures; as all the materials are ridged, except the seaweeds, care must be taken to check the design if you wish to avoid too deep a frame. The depth of the frame is governed by the depth of the arrangement. With dried materials there is a little 'give', though the glass should never press on anything in a picture, but in the case of shells it will crack or break them.

An easy way of checking on this while you are making the design, is to have a box lid with an inch-deep edge. Put the arranged design into the lid before it is stuck, and lay a ruler across from edge to edge, sliding it over the design. If it clears everything all is well, if not either alter the angle of the shells that project, or plan to have a deeper-sided basic frame.

(6) Box framing

This special method of framing is necessary if these pictures are to be preserved, unchanged and undimmed as mine are after very many years. Few people are aware of how much dirt there is in the air of the cleanest home. If any member of the family smokes a lot, or parties are given where smoking is the rule rather than the exception, then a brown film floats over everything. Just run a finger over the glass of a picture after such an occasion and you will be surprised to see the brown stain that results.

This method of framing cannot be inexpensive because it is virtually two frames, one fitting on top of the other, with the glass held in between (see diagram, page 54), either with a special glue or with very fine picture nails. The resulting box frame preserves the picture perfectly from dirt and atmospheric changes.

But do not despair, there are ways of economizing. The best of these is to have a handy husband or son, who can be persuaded to make the basic under-frame for you. This is made of a plain sloping moulding, not less than an inch deep. It is easy to find at most Do-It-Yourself shops, where home decorators are catered for. When the basic frame has been made to fit your picture, take it to a frame-maker and ask him to make and fix on the top frame, which should be made of an ornamental moulding to suit the picture. These decorative mouldings can also be bought at some Do-It-Yourself shops, but only in eight- to ten-feet lengths. This would mean that all your pictures would have the same top framing, which might not always be suitable to the picture.

When you go to the frame-maker, whether with a basic frame or to have the complete box-frame made, take your picture with you so that you can select the moulding which will set it off to the best advantage. Always keep the picture in a box or blown-up polythene bag until it has been framed, and don't leave it at the shop. In fact they will usually prefer you not to, as there is a risk of it being damaged by somebody accidentally putting something heavy on top of it.

Many a gardener would envy these flowers.

FRAMING

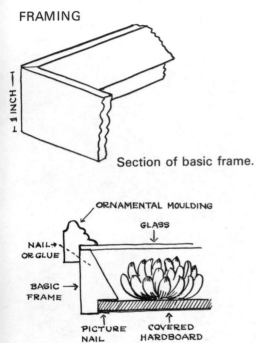

Section of basic frame.

ORNAMENTAL MOULDING

GLASS

NAIL→ OR GLUE

BASIC → FRAME

PICTURE NAIL

COVERED HARDBOARD

Section showing glass held in place on top of basic frame by ornamental moulding.

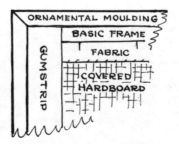

ORNAMENTAL MOULDING

BASIC FRAME

FABRIC

GUMSTRIP

COVERED HARDBOARD

PICTURE BACK
Showing sealing with gumstrip when 'buttons' are not used.

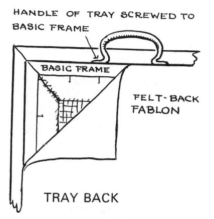

HANDLE OF TRAY SCREWED TO
BASIC FRAME

BASIC FRAME

FELT-BACK
FABLON

TRAY BACK

Another, and very easy way of economizing, is to have one complete box frame made and ask for 'buttons' to be put on the back. This is the name by which clips are known in the trade. In this way, providing that you make all your pictures the same size, one frame will serve many pictures. All you have to do is move the clips aside, then slide a blunt knife round the edge of the picture, gently levering it out of the frame.

You can then change the picture as often as you like, according to your whim or the time of year, but always store the unframed pictures in boxes and in blown-up polythene bags, as protection against a damp atmosphere. A pleasant idea would be a picture for every season of the year, with backgrounds of blues or greens for spring and summer, gold or russet shades for the autumn, and glowing orange or rosy reds for winter, and all for the price of one frame!

Also keep a look out at jumble sales and on market stalls. You may see a frame with a plain sloping moulding for sale quite cheaply, and if you take out the probably hideous picture, and have an attractive top moulding added, replacing the picture with one of your own, you will have a bargain.

These pictures also make very attractive trays, not for heavy things, but for serving drinks. The method of framing is exactly the same, but the covered board must be held in place with fine picture nails, and then the back sealed over with felt-backed Fablon. Small handles of wood or metal are added on the short sides (see diagram, page 55).

Large pictures, with 'feet' added to the bottom of the frame, make beautiful firescreens, filling the empty hearth with a permanent arrangement of dust-proof flowers.

And remember, the only big expense is the last expense. Everything else is free or very inexpensive, so have fun, and even if you don't think you can make a picture, try! When giving classes I have been constantly pleased and surprised at the results achieved by people who diffidently declared that they had no artistic talent at all. It is the kind of people who have the wisdom and ability to learn from any mistakes that they make, who soon find themselves achieving proficiency in a remarkably short space of time.

The flowers are gone but they bloom again with a fairy-like delicacy.

(7) A few hints and thoughts

I said at the beginning of this book that part of the fun was hunting for the materials. Well, having found them start a 'bank', but keep it in a dry place, not an outhouse. Whatever the materials of your art or craft, correct storage is necessary, from oil paints to clay. The atmosphere can be too hot or too damp, so when looking for a storage place do bear these things in mind. I am old-fashioned, my 'banks' are kept under the bed, and if any burglar is also so old-fashioned as to try and hide there, he will be hard put to find any room.

Store the dried materials in dress or shoe boxes, or an old suit-case, with layers of tissue paper in between the various kinds of leaves, flowers and seed heads, putting the flatter and heavier things in the bottom layer.

When you return from your holiday sort out the different kinds of shells, and store them in small labelled boxes. Have rather larger boxes for the fascinating bits of flotsam and jetsam, and another for seaweeds. Then when you have the time to start a picture you will know exactly where to find the different items you want.

I don't wait till I get back from my holiday, but go armed with suit-able small boxes, and wash and sort my shells while I am still away. There are always so many calls on one's time once home again. Besides it is an ideal occupation while basking on the beach. Interesting without being strenuous, moreover the children will often enjoy helping, and it will keep them happy and occupied. It also provides a chance to make up any deficiency in either numbers or selection, of either shells or seaweeds.

I am always on the look-out for useful boxes for storing shells, and have found that quite a few very good ones come with the groceries and general shopping. Both the large and small containers of soft cheeses and soft margarine are just right for storing shells. Notelet boxes and the bigger chocolate boxes are good for keeping seaweeds, and other odds and ends. Cough lozenge tins are only

Gentle, curving drifting charm.

useful for beads and sequins as they are made of metal. All these boxes can then be fitted into a suitcase so that your seashore items are all together, and readily available when you want them.

Also keep a small collection of fabric remnants in as varied a range of colours and shades as possible. It is maddening to want to start a picture, only to find that you have nothing suitable for the background.

Kept this way your 'bank' won't take up too much room, which as few of us live in large houses is very important. Not many architects seem to think much about either storage space or room for hobbies when planning a house, though both are basic to comfortable and happy living.

So with all your treasures in a 'bank', perhaps on some dreary winter day when you have a little spare time, there they will be waiting for you, waiting to be made into lovely glowing pictures. And if the day started by feeling dreary it won't end that way, whatever the weather or time of year, for there is no better mental tonic and pleasure than creating something of lasting loveliness.

If the materials used in these pictures seem too humble for such aspirations, always remember that most of the materials used for painting, sculpture and pottery are also of the earth, and it is the skill of the artist or craftsman that can change these simple things into objects of enduring beauty. The clay remains the same, only the potters differ.

Interesting details are blended into a harmonious design.

(8) Fun for children

Here are just a few ideas for things that children can make with shells, starting with one for very young children, and progressing to ones for children of ten or twelve. But of course it is not possible to be rigid about age-groups, some children seem to be born with more brains in their hands, and some with more or only brains in their heads.

First the pictures that can be made on the *rough* side of the hardboard by quite young children.

You must of course protect the floor or table with lots of newspaper, or better still an old sheet of polythene, as this protects against spilt water as well.

The only assistance that you will need to give is mixing relays of fresh Polyfilla, though the children may soon get the hang of doing this themselves. Explain to them that it dries rather quickly, and that once the mixture has dried up it can't be used, and a fresh mixture must be made.

As they will be working with the board flat on the floor or table, and to give them longer to work the shells into place, I would recommend a softer and therefore wetter mixture than the soft butter consistency suggested in Chapter 5. It is best to mix the Polyfilla in an old plastic cup so that it can't be broken.

With an old teaspoon, they can scoop the Polyfilla onto the rough-sided surface of the hardboard, and press the shells into it, just as they please. They can either fill the board with shells, or make a selective pattern; the earlier the age the more completely will the board be covered as a rule.

When it is quite dry, and this will take a little longer than usual because of the wetter mixture, and the depth of the Polyfilla spooned onto the board, they can then paint all over the shells and the board too with gold or silver paint. Other colours can be used,

Restful and harmonious in its simplicity.

but these are usually the most popular. I don't advise spraying as this is difficult for small hands to manage. When it is dry, father can be asked to screw a metal picture hanger onto the back, and it can be hung with pride in the sitting room, or on their bedroom wall. The second idea is a shell garden on an old plastic plate. It will make a very pretty table decoration, especially if a light blue or green one is available. Again your part will be small, just rub the plate hard with coarse sandpaper; this enables the Polyfilla to 'key-in' with both the shells and the plate. These gardens can also be made on unglazed tiles, but the underside should be covered with Fablon to prevent furniture or woodwork from being scratched.

Your only other job may be mixing Polyfilla, but this time it needs to be mixed to a soft butter consistency, because to get the prettiest effects some of the shells must stand up as if they were flowers. Perhaps a short path of Polyfilla, covered with bits of broken shell, could lead up to a cockle shell, placed to look like a small ornamental pool (see diagram).

Again a spoon is needed to spread the Polyfilla onto the plate, and if they are old enough, also a blunt knife or a plastic one—these can usually be bought at a toy shop. The knife is needed in case the young artist gets exciting ideas such as sticking shells on shells, which will need small quantities of Polyfilla to stick them in place, and for this something less clumsy than a spoon will be necessary.

(Opposite)
Garden, field, woods and hedgerow meet in this picture with sequins used to evoke the idea of dew glistening in the early sun-shine. The seedheads of the clematis tangutica are set with hair lacquer and the barley awn is stuck so that it looks as if it is blowing in the wind.

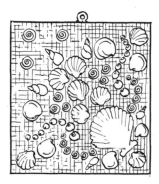

This is more of a design than most young children would make. It is shown here to set their imaginations working.

Plate garden of shells.

Box for dressing-table or bathroom.

(Opposite)
Here the 'wave' line is done by bleaching, and the flowers drift on soft lines in shades of green. Oyster shell flowers have bead-headed stamens surrounding a periwinkle centre. The other flowers are made of Atlantic coquina in every shade of coral, with tiny orange scallop shells added. Dark brown seaweed provides branches on which the flowers can rest.

Two children I know made these gardens when they were seven and nine years old, with very pretty results, and very little help from me; in fact all I did was to sandpaper the plates. Again plenty of newspaper or polythene is needed as protective covering.

The last three things that I am going to suggest may only be suitable for the slightly older child, say about twelve years old. They can also be made by grown-ups, but in the first one to be described, a different fixative should be used if the result is to be 100 per cent lasting and resistant to water.

The first of the three are little shell pots for cactus, and other very small plants. Deep, as well as large shells are necessary for the pot part, and for this both cockle and venus shells are good. The lower part or stand, can be made of a matching shell, placed in a reverse position, or two or three smaller shells stuck together to make the base (see diagram). Test out either the group of shells or the one shell used for a base by balancing the big 'pot' shell on the base. If a group is being used these must be stuck together first. When they are dry some more Polyfilla should be added to the centre of the group, and also a little to the big 'pot' shell at the point where it will rest on the base. The Polyfilla will grip better if all the shells are made slightly damp.

Do the same thing when one reversed shell is used as a base, except that a bigger lump of Polyfilla will be needed on the bottom shell to keep the two shells balanced. This extra Polyfilla will show, but can be concealed by sticking a few small shells round the joining point (see diagram).

If you want to make these with a completely waterproof fixative, follow the same method but use Bostik wall-tile adhesive in place of Polyfilla. I have made them for bazaars with little cactus mamillaria growing in them, and they have sold very well. Some small rock plants can also be grown in these pots; I have used Arenaria and the dwarf dianthus.

Shell pot made from two shells glued together.

Pot with base of three shells.

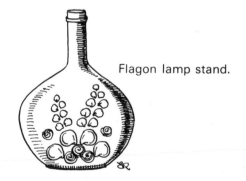

Flagon lamp stand.

The second is a variation of something that one often sees made, a bottle covered all over with shells and used as a lamp holder. If instead of an ordinary bottle you can find a flagon, it will have two advantages, a bigger and therefore better balanced base, and flat sides which will give scope for sticking the shells in a design, or to resemble a spray of flowers. For this reason I suggest that it may be something more suitable for an older child to attempt.

Lay the bottle on one of the flat sides and arrange the shells, marking the design on the glass with a pencil crayon. UHU is the better fixative in this case, and if it goes over the sides of the shells a little, it will not show on glass. All the shells should be stuck with the curved side uppermost. The fixative is run round their inside edge, and they are then stuck into place. Leave the bottle lying flat until the glue is quite dry, before attempting the other side. When the decoration of the other side is begun, lay the already ornamented side on two or three layers of old towelling to protect it from damage.

The third of this group of ideas varies with the kind of plastic boxes that can be bought. A well-known chain of chemists used to keep a very good range, including screw-topped powder boxes, but these are now difficult to find; one branch may still have some and not another. They do, however, stock a pleasant-shaped jar with a lid, designed to hold dentures, which may not sound very prepossessing. But with a pattern of shells, stuck round the central knob of the lid, and a few sequins added, it would make an attractive box for all those odds and ends that frequently clutter up a dressing-table (see diagram, page 65). Again use UHU as a fixative.

Earthenware jugs, flower pots, etc, can all be decorated with shells, but must only be used indoors if Polyfilla is used, as it will not withstand constant soaking with rain.

A black oyster shell flower, dark seaweed and orange
'butterflies' drift on blue-green waves.

The stamens have triple turquoise blue heads, and the 'butterflies'
heads of blue-green sequins.

Appendix

Recipe for making skeleton leaves

Mature leaves must be used, that is ones that have turned brown, but only certain kinds have the fibrous vein structure that enables them to turn into what we call skeleton leaves. Amongst those that can are ivy, holly, lime, magnolia and several kinds of poplar. Magnolias skeletonise so easily that they can often be found under the bush or tree in late autumn, so they may not be worth doing.

Use a very old saucepan, and put into it only as many leaves as you will have time to skim. This is quite a delicate job and cannot be hurried, so probably twelve leaves are enough, especially if it is your first attempt. Cover with two pints of cold water, add a handful of common washing soda, bring to simmering point and keep there for two hours.

Do not remove the leaves all at once, as they are very difficult to skim when they have dried at all. So take them out one by one, lay them flat on a piece of newspaper, and scrape off the slimy brown covering with a blunt knife. Do this very carefully, always starting at the stalk end. Turn the leaf over and scrape the other side, then rinse well in cold water and lay out on blotting paper to dry. This must be done very slowly or the leaves will curl up at the edges.

Bleach can be added to the last rinsing water at the rate of one tablespoon to a pint, and the leaves left in this till sufficient change has taken place, but it does tend to make them brittle unless extra slow and cool conditions are used in drying. In this case they should be placed between two layers of blotting paper.